D1480323

Louisiana Journey

Louisiana Journey

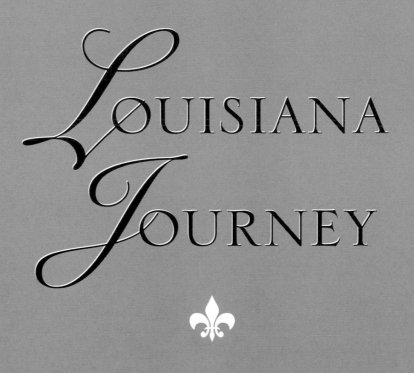

Photographs and Text by
Neil Johnson

Louisiana State University Press
Baton Rouge and London

ACKNOWLEDGMENTS

The author wishes to acknowledge his gratitude to the wonderful team at LSU Press and to the following individuals and other entities who went above and beyond to help make this book possible:

ASMP Gulf South chapter
Dot Bassett
Major Jim Beinkemper
Don Bell
Gordon Boogaerts
Robert & Jan White Brantley
George Broach
Bill Cook
Bobby DeBlieux
Jay Dugas
Garber Farms
Dale Garber
Charles Godchaux
Bill Goulet
John Hebert
Ibra January
Richard & Jesse Johnson
Mike & Norma Kilgore
Bruce & March Kingsdorf
The Lake Arthur Club
Murray Lloyd
Louisiana Endowment for the Humanities
John & Sarah Luster
Leland McCullough
Patric McWilliams
Peter Main
Dan & Deenie Reese
Jonathan Reynolds
Steve & Martha Strohschein
Jason Summerlin
Texaco, Inc.
Mary Jack Wald
David & Kerry Yeattes

Copyright © 1997 by Neil Johnson
All rights reserved
Manufactured in Hong Kong

06 05 04 03 02 01 00 99 98   5 4 3 2

Designer: Laura Roubique Gleason
Typeface: Minion with Serlio and Snell Roundhand display
Printer and binder: Everbest Printing Co. through Four Colour Imports, Ltd., Louisville, Kentucky

Library of Congress Cataloging-in-Publication Data

Johnson, Neil, 1954–
    Louisiana journey / photographs and text by Neil Johnson.
        p.   cm.
    Includes index.
    ISBN 0-8071-2229-7 (alk. paper)
    1. Louisiana—Pictorial works.   2. Louisiana—Description and travel.   I. Title.
    F370.J65 1997
    917.6304'63'0222—dc21   97-26862
                                                                  CIP

The paper in this book meets the guidelines for permanence and durability of the Committee on Production Guidelines for Book Longevity of the Council on Library Resources. ∞

To my mother,
Lea Morton Johnson,
a Massachusetts transplant to
Louisiana who, with her Yankee
pragmatism intact, personifies southern
generosity, charm, and grace, and who
passed on to me the very dominant
gene for loving books

INTRODUCTION

*M*y Louisiana Journey began by train.

My father's father was a quarterback for LSU way back when the quarterback's unassuming job was simply to take the ball and hand it to the running back. He handed to me my first memory of the state outside of my hometown of Shreveport by taking my brother and me on the game train from Shreveport to Baton Rouge to see an LSU football game. I was only eight and impressed as any eight-year-old would be at being on a train full of boisterously enthusiastic football fans and then by the awesome experience of 50-yard-line seats at Tiger Stadium on Saturday night. It's too bad the game train doesn't run anymore; even the station in downtown Shreveport is history. But for my journey of exploration and discovery throughout this incredible state, it was a dynamic beginning.

In 1967 the inimitable Manelle Weaver introduced my seventh-grade class at Southfield School to Iberville, Audubon, and Huey. She then courageously boarded a bus with us to guide us across the landscape these men once walked. Memories of that four-day swing through the state still resonate within me, especially the frightening experience with a larger-than-life alligator at Avery Island, the exotic French menu at Antoine's in the Quarter, and falling in love with architecture for the first time at Shadows-on-the-Teche. Mrs. Weaver gave me a generous B+ on my Louisiana Project Book. I give her an A+ for her teaching skills.

But to understand a place, one must leave it. In between adolescence and adulthood, I spent four years studying in Virginia and have since traveled from Maine to Hawaii and from Florida to Alaska. And after circling the globe, my feelings were confirmed: Louisiana is unique.

My chosen profession as photographer and writer may have trained me to observe and record, but it is curiosity that drives me. And, yes, this is one curious state. If Louisiana were to arrive at a family gathering of states, it would be as the eccentric uncle who told colorful stories about unlikely adventures that would captivate the children and set the adults to shaking their heads. But the gleam in his eye and the fire in his voice would hold everyone spellbound for hours and leave them asking for more. The family would roll its collective eyes at times, but then be proud to tears at other times. Boring he would not be.

How fortunate that *Louisiana Life* magazine was born at the end of 1980, the exact time I became a very naïve freelance photographer. It needed another shooter to help fill its glossy pages, and I needed a sponsor to send me out to explore Louisiana. With its backing, I was privileged to witness the birth of several thoroughbred horses, to ride an M-1 tank at Fort Polk, and to fly my first aerobatic barrel roll. The editor, Nancy Marshall, even assigned me to walk the Great Wall of China, but that's another story.

I am from north Louisiana's "I-20 corridor," a part of the state with its own beauty and energy and history and opportunity. The north was populated by settlers on their way from the Carolinas and points east to Texas and points west. The houses of worship up here are primarily Protestant, and our spirits tend to be a bit more sedate than those of south Louisianians. But I hope I have been able to portray a part of the population that, although sometimes feeling left out of the state dance, still has a deep love for all that is Louisiana—and makes good use of I-49 to head south now and again to give ourselves over to the charms of Acadiana, the River Road, and St. Charles Avenue.

What have I learned along my journey? For starters, the essence of Louisiana is water. So much of what makes this one of the most fascinating of states emanates from its bayous, rivers, lakes, the Gulf, and that huge hybrid part of the state that is not quite land, not quite water. Waterways were the primary mode of early transportation. Louisiana's people either arrived by water and went no farther or they arrived via land but hesitated permanently at river crossings. Many realized that the water would be their source of sustenance and maybe even fortune, and so they stuck close to it. It is the eons of river flooding that have made the land so fertile. And from this well-watered landscape and from the open water itself comes a bounty of food the envy of the world. And from its people—with a complex history of both exultant celebration and immeasurable pain—music pours forth in a ceaseless flow. Jazz, Cajun and zydeco, blues, rock and roll—all were either formed from scratch here or were heavily influenced from within these borders.

And finally, this state is birds. Most of the more distinguished species of North America live here or winter here. With its extensive forests and wetlands, Louisiana must be bird paradise. If I tend to preach now and then about preserving these habitats—especially the wetlands—it is because I've fallen in love with these winged neighbors and visitors.

Water, food, music, birds. Louisiana.

In the planning of this project and then during the editing process, I avoided the overly familiar. For example, I had to include the beloved Shadows-on-the-Teche, yet I chose not to present its familiar facade. When simply overwhelmed by the power of a time-tested image, I tried to put some kind of twist on it. I photographed Oak Alley many ways but kept returning to the classic view from the levee and ended up capturing it at sunrise on a Christmas morning. It was important to me to include im-

ages of the little-known but huge Dolet Hills coal mine. And just down the road, I bothered International Paper until they finally allowed me to bring a camera into their world-class Mansfield paper mill to illustrate in a small way what they do with all those pine trees.

Each of these images is a gift. Many single images within these pages are the result of days of correspondence, phone calls, preparation, travel, and finally location work that included exposing many rolls of film. When one transparency raises itself above the rest and cries out, "Use me!"—the sunrise over the marshes of Rainey Refuge or the two ballet dancers in Monroe's ELsong Gardens—I am thrilled. But it is still a gift.

Other images were handed to me fortuitously and spontaneously along the road, such as the great egret carrying the fish and the boy holding the crawfish. My eyes were always searching and my camera was always loaded for such visual gifts because they are so damned fleeting. And yet, as any photographer knows, these images present themselves in a truly constant flow.

To photograph a subject as large as a state can only mean frustration. There were so many images I missed due to inappropriate light. So many where the clock or calendar or mileage became my insurmountable enemy. So many clearly previewed in my imagination but elusive in my viewfinder. These images—a seemingly infinite number, of every conceivable subject—were either left behind forever or left with a blessing for other photographers to capture.

It is my hope and prayer that this book will not take the place of anyone's actual journeys but will inspire exploration. And, as T. S. Eliot wrote:

> We shall not cease from exploration.
> And the end of all our exploring
> Will be to arrive where we started
> And know the place for the first time.

LOUISIANA JOURNEY

With the Mississippi River under control, agriculture has taken over most of what was once 25 million acres of seasonally flooded hardwood bottomlands. The 5 million remaining acres scattered along the Mississippi valley include the Tensas River Wildlife Refuge in southern Madison and northern Tensas Parishes, where palmetto fronds such as these flourish.

For years I have been drawn to Poverty Point, the prehistoric site north of I-20 near the town of Epps in West Carroll Parish. It's a little out of the way, but a good mystery awaits.

Sometime around 1500 B.C., the people here began a task that would take generations to complete. Hauling dirt in baskets, they piled up tens of millions of basketloads. Eventually they created what were, at the time, the largest manmade objects in the hemisphere. One mound measures more than two football fields in length and width and rises to the height of a seven-story building. It faces a stairstep series of crescent-shaped terraces, the widest three-quarters of a mile across.

Although less than 1 percent of the large site, designated as the Poverty Point State Commemorative Area, has been excavated for study, more than 100,000 artifacts, including the spearpoints shown here, have been recovered. Yet archaeologists can only speculate about who these people were and what, exactly, was the purpose of their vast earthworks. Nor is their fate known, beyond the fact that around 800 B.C. they and their way of life vanished forever.

Standing atop the largest mound, it is difficult to imagine what a person might have seen there 3,000 years ago. Crowds of worshipers? A village of carefully aligned mud huts? A teeming bazaar? Or . . . or what? We simply do not know.

Today, the view is obstructed by trees that remain uncut for an important reason: their roots have helped to hold the mound together for eons, protecting it from erosion for us to stand upon it and wonder.

Facing page: Christ Episcopal Church in St. Joseph on the Mississippi River was built in 1872. The builder, a man named Hennessey, is said to have worked from his memory of English parish churches, although here he executed in wood the Gothic details that in England would normally have been done in brick or stone.

Spearpoints, Poverty Point State Commemorative Area.

The late Emy-Lou Biedenharn, opera singer, arts patron, and Monroe native, devoted her later years to setting up the Emy-Lou Biedenharn Foundation, to which she eventually donated her home, ELsong, and its formal gardens.

The Twin City Ballet, founded in 1970 by artistic director Linda Ford, has an active performance schedule for Monroe, West Monroe, and the northeast Louisiana region. The company has performed on occasion in the ELsong Gardens.

The annual Christmas Boat Flotilla lights up the Ouachita River at Monroe.

Adjacent to ELsong, the Biedenharn Foundation's Bible Research Center, founded by Emy-Lou Biedenharn in 1971, contains a nondenominational museum and a library for biblical studies. The center presents regular exhibits of its collection of biblical texts and artifacts, including these antique and rare Bibles.

Facing page: Poultry production (broilers and eggs) is second in dollar value only to timber in Louisiana's agricultural output. Concentrated mainly north and west of Natchitoches, "broiler houses" turn out hybrid chickens, bred for quick growth, that are ready for processing in six to nine weeks. The operation shown here is outside of Farmerville in Union Parish.

Monroe's Forsythe Park is home to the popular sculpture *Dragonfly in the Park.*

The ranching of ostriches and emus is one of Louisiana's newest agribusinesses, with most of the hundreds of ranches located in the northern half of the state. This one is outside West Monroe.

Overleaf: Smokehouse east of Farmerville.

Ruston peaches, long known for their quality, size, and taste, are now grown by only a small fraction of the commercial farms that made them famous. Since the late 1970s, when Ruston-area peach farming peaked, several devastating late-spring freezes have discouraged many farmers from growing peaches, which normally do well in the hilly north Louisiana landscape.

The well-traveled Grambling State University Tiger Marching Band not only carries a widely respected musical legacy, but also provides a way for its young musicians to see the world. Started in 1952 by Ralph Waldo Emerson Jones—who used credit from Sears to buy the first instruments—the band today continues its rich halftime and parade tradition on football fields and streets throughout the country.

A deer hunter in Bienville Parish sleeps off an unsuccessful early morning hunt.

On a lonely stretch of road near this bullet-riddled marker just south of Mt. Lebanon in Bienville Parish, a posse of lawmen lay in ambush on May 23, 1934. When the Ford Deluxe sedan carrying Clyde Barrow and Bonnie Parker arrived at the spot, it was greeted by a torrent of gunfire, putting a violent end to the couple's infamous crime spree.

The Greek-revival Claiborne Parish Courthouse in Homer was completed in 1861 and is one of only four surviving pre–Civil War courthouses in the state.

Champion watermelon, Haynesville, Claiborne Parish.

New fern growth at Caney Lakes Recreation Area, north of Minden.

Cockfighting is a centuries-old legal sport widely
followed in many rural areas in both north and
south Louisiana. Game roosters such as this one
near Plain Dealing are bred solely for fighting.

Facing page: The Red River Valley's combination of
fertile soil and hot, dry growing season makes it
one of the most productive areas in the whole cotton belt. These pickers are working a field in
Caddo Parish not far from the Arkansas border.

Home of the American Rose Society, the shady gardens of the American Rose Center spread out under forty-two acres of tall pines just west of Shreveport. The largest American garden dedicated to roses, the center nurtures over 20,000 roses of more than 400 varieties.

Overleaf: Shreveport was founded on the Red River in 1835 after Captain Henry Miller Shreve cleared a 100-mile-long logjam, making the river navigable for transporting cotton and other goods, as well as people. The city is the cultural and business center of the Ark-La-Tex, comprising northwest Louisiana, southwest Arkansas, and east Texas.

Facing page: Roughnecks on a drilling rig floor in Caddo Parish work to change a drill bit. New technology has helped bring about a resurgence in Louisiana's oil and gas industry, partly by reopening old fields, but it seems doubtful that the state will ever return to the opulent glory days before the mid-1980s price downturn.

The Shreveport skyline provides a backdrop for the SporTran Center, the hub of the mass transit system for Shreveport and Bossier City. The structure, with its fiberglass-reinforced Teflon fabric canopy, is essentially a high-tech tent.

Facing page: Organized hot air ballooning in Louisiana began in Hammond, but it was the U.S. National Hot Air Balloon Championships held from 1989 through 1991 in Baton Rouge that sparked statewide interest in the sport. Large annual events are now held in Baton Rouge, Lafayette, and Shreveport. Pictured is Shreveport's Red River Rally.

The southern magnolia is Louisiana's state flower.

The Shreveport Assembly Plant of General Motors'
Truck Group, which began operations in 1981,
manufactures Chevrolet and GMC small pickup
trucks. It also makes trucks for Isuzu and was the
first GM plant to produce electric-powered trucks.

Facing page: The Strand Theater was opened in
downtown Shreveport in 1925 as a movie palace
and vaudeville theater by Julian and A. D. Saenger
and Simon Ehrlich. The Strand was the flagship
theater of the renowned Saenger Brothers theater
chain, which included over 300 theaters in the U.S.
and Caribbean. It was acquired, restored, and re-
opened in its former grandeur in 1984 by the non-
profit Strand Theater Corporation, which now
runs it as a hall for the performing arts.

Riverboat traffic on the Red River ceased at the beginning of the twentieth century and reappeared in the 1990s with the completion of the Red River Navigation project and the advent of riverboat casinos. Harrah's Casino Shreveport was the first of what is now a small fleet of riverboat casinos providing twenty-four-hour dockside gambling in Shreveport and Bossier City. The advent of this huge new industry in 1994 sparked a transformation of the riverfronts of both cities. Shown here is the Isle of Capri Casino in Bossier City.

Bossier City's Barksdale Air Force Base is the headquarters of the 8th Air Force, the 2d Bomb Wing (which flies B-52H bombers) and the 917th Fighter Wing Air Force Reserve. With 22,000 acres of Bossier Parish land purchased from sales of a 1929 Shreveport bond issue and donated to the U.S. Army, the War Department dedicated what was then known as Barksdale Field in 1933.

Facing page: Near Lake Bistineau in Bossier Parish.

Louisiana's trees bring in more money by far than any other agricultural product. Commercial forests in almost every corner of the state provide a large and renewable source of lumber and paper products. This forest is undergoing harvest thinning in south Bossier Parish.

Overleaf: In the spring of 1864, Union troops began the Red River campaign, aimed at capturing Shreveport—the state's Confederate capital at the time—and driving on into Texas. On April 8, a Confederate army met the advancing Federals just south of Mansfield. After a fierce battle, the Union force retreated and regrouped at Pleasant Hill, where a heavy but inconclusive fight occurred the next day. Although the Confederates withdrew northward, the Union commander decided to break off the campaign. Each spring at the Mansfield State Commemorative Area, a reenactment is staged to observe the anniversary of the battles.

Facing page: The little town of Keatchie in De Soto Parish boasts three churches—Baptist, Presbyterian, and Methodist—over one hundred years old. This one, decorated for Christmas, is the Keatchie Methodist Church, built during the late 1850s.

International Paper's Mansfield Mill every day produces more than 4,000 tons of paper to be shipped all over the world and manufactured into corrugated cardboard boxes.

A massive electric-powered dragline with its 320-foot-long boom scoops away topsoil to reach a seam of lignite coal at the 30,000-acre Dolet Hills mine in south De Soto Parish. The low-grade coal goes to the nearby Dolet Hills Power Plant, where it is burned to produce electricity for use in Louisiana, Arkansas, Texas, and Oklahoma. Each year about 300 acres of land are mined and then reclaimed for forestry.

Facing page: Interstate 49 near Pleasant Hill.

What was once Briarwood Plantation in northern Natchitoches Parish is now also known as the Caroline Dormon Nature Preserve, named for the legendary forest conservationist whose home the plantation was. Dormon, instrumental in establishing the Kisatchie National Forest in Louisiana, became widely known for her vast knowledge of native plants. Long after her death in 1971, the preserve continues to be used as an outdoor classroom for the study of Louisiana nature. Pictured above are native bog torch blooms, also known as golden club.

Spring assails Louisiana with flowers and an intense green among the oaks, pines, and cypresses. Bearing witness to this silent explosion from a canoe on Saline Bayou is a distinct treat.

This sleepy bayou in the Kisatchie National Forest northeast of Natchitoches is the state's sole representative in the National Scenic River System, but it is as far from being a river as smoky jazz is from rock and roll. It is slow and serene and could care less in which direction its water lazily digresses. Under the enveloping trees, voices are hushed. It is a place that makes its own music.

Even the great blue herons don't like to cut straight across the bends like crows, preferring instead to fly the serpentine course of the bayou as if they, too, were taking the scenic route.

We slowly follow them, our craft as noiseless as the birds' wings.

Saline Bayou National Scenic River.

Winnfield is the seat of Winn Parish, from which came three governors—Huey Long, O. K. Allen, and Earl Long—who set the populist political tone of Louisiana's government from the 1920s into the 1970s. The town is the home of the Louisiana Political Museum and Political Hall of Fame.

Hunting wild hogs has a long tradition in central Louisiana, where even Governor Earl K. Long took an active interest. Instrumental to the hunt is the state dog, the Catahoula hound, also known as the Catahoula stock dog, the Catahoula hog dog, the Catahoula leopard dog (for its often mottled or spotted coat), and the Catahoula cur. At Uncle Earl's Hog Dog Trials, held in Winnfield each spring, Catahoulas from around the U.S. compete at herding wild pigs.

Facing page: At harvest time, cotton is trucked to gins like this one near Powhatan, where the "sucker pipe" pulls it inside to be cleaned, separated from the seeds, and pressed into bales.

In 1714, Governor Antoine de la Mothe Cadillac of the French colony of Louisiana sent Louis Juchereau de St.-Denis to establish a trading post at the Natchitoches Indian village on what was then the Red River. Before continuing on as a trade emissary to the Spanish in Mexico, St.-Denis constructed Fort St. Jean Baptiste to guard the western boundary of Louisiana for the French. He returned in 1722 and remained as fort commandant until his death in 1744. Natchitoches, which developed around the French post, survived, making it the oldest permanent European settlement within the Louisiana Purchase. This replica, built from the actual 1732 plans of the fort, is open to the public and offers a busy schedule of living-history events throughout the year.

The Creole buildings of Natchitoches' brick Front
Street, overlooking Cane River Lake, reflect the
warm glow of Christmas lights during the whole
month of December. The Natchitoches Christmas
Festival, begun in 1926, attracts throngs of people
to the riverfront area for fireworks and the switch-
ing on of the lights.

Melrose Plantation, south of Natchitoches, has a remarkable history, having been owned and developed by freed slaves long before the Civil War. Begun in the late 1700s, it grew out of the determination and enterprise of a freed slave woman known as Coincoin (pronounced koh-kwi) and her many children, ten of whom took the last name, Metoyer, of their white planter father. In the early 1900s, under other owners, Melrose became famous as an artists' colony. Pictured is the "Big House," completed in 1833. The two hexagonal *garçonnières* were added in 1908. The term is from the French *garçon,* "boy." On plantations it referred to separate quarters for the young, unmarried men of the place.

Once a cook for Melrose Plantation, the late Clementine Hunter became one of the South's most acclaimed primitive artists. Upstairs at Melrose Plantation's African House, a structure reminiscent of the straw-thatched houses of West Africa, one can see murals of Hunter's plantation-life scenes.

Facing page: Named for the Cherokee rose, the Cherokee Plantation home is an example of pure West Indies Creole architecture. The home was built by Emile Sompayrac in 1839 just south of Natchitoches. Cherokee roses still grow on the property.

For many years, Louisiana's plentiful rivers and bayous were the primary avenues of transportation. One of the least reliable of these waterways was the Red River, shallow, full of sandbars, prone to logjams, and frequently shifting its course. The Red was stabilized in 1994 with the opening of the J. Bennett Johnston Waterway. The project includes five locks and dams between the Mississippi River and Shreveport, allowing for barge traffic, among the most economical methods of transporting bulk cargoes.

In the early twentieth century, clear-cut logging over vast areas of Louisiana removed most of the state's virgin longleaf pine. Little reforestation took place until the Civilian Conservation Corps began replanting pines during the 1930s. Meanwhile, naturalist Caroline Dormon had initiated a movement that resulted in the creation of the Kisatchie National Forest in 1930. (*Kisatchie* is from an Indian word generally thought to mean "long cane.") Today the longleaf is being reintroduced to its natural range here in the Kisatchie Ranger District, south of Natchitoches.

The Toledo Bend Reservoir was created in 1968 by damming the Sabine River. The water-conservation project, jointly owned by Texas and Louisiana, was built totally without federal funding. Toledo Bend today is a lake known for game fishing, especially for striped and largemouth bass.

Widespread destruction of forest habitat through logging and agriculture at the beginning of the twentieth century greatly depleted the North American white-tailed deer throughout Louisiana. A. J. Hodges, Sr., pioneer conservationist and timber manager, was instrumental in restocking the deer in the western region. Now prolific throughout the state, they roam Louisiana's woods, fields, and marshes freely until November, when hunting season begins.

Overleaf: Hodges Gardens, the nation's largest privately owned horticultural parkland and wildlife preserve, is the legacy of A. J. Hodges and his wife, Nona Trigg Hodges. The centerpiece of the park's 4,700 acres, twelve miles south of Many, is an abandoned stone quarry, which the couple transformed into formal gardens. Opened to the public in 1956, the park surrounds a 225-acre lake and includes picnic areas, a scenic drive, and hiking trails.

$\mathcal{W}\!e$ arise from our Humvee bed at 4 A.M., before any hint of daylight struggles through the pines deep in the backwoods of Fort Polk. My Joint Readiness Training Center host freshens up the green paint on his face, and we head down the road quietly on foot to the wooded defensive position where we watched soldiers digging in the day before. Suddenly a simulated artillery barrage begins in the woods to our left. Between thunderous explosions, Jim whispers for me to remain as quiet as possible.

The clearing is now dimly lit with the colorless aura of a newborn overcast morning. The position appears totally deserted; all evidence of human presence is hidden below ground or camouflaged. A mockingbird sings.

Part of me wants to crouch and hide to watch what is about to happen, but we continue to walk upright through the position. My mind tells me that almost a hundred anxious men are within earshot of a loud whisper. This group is based in Hawaii. They are far, far from home. For the time being, everyone is silent and invisible.

An equally invisible but much more experienced "enemy" hunkers down in the nearby forest awaiting the word to attack. Soon the still air will be laden with the repeated pops from blank cartridges—each report accompanied by an invisible laser beam aimed at the sensors worn by the soldier in the gunsight.

Purple smoke will billow across the clearing. Slowly the enemy will advance until finally, without opposition, tanks will rumble out of the underbrush, up the dirt road, and on into the morning.

The U.S. Army will have suffered the loss of this position. But, oh, the lessons learned.

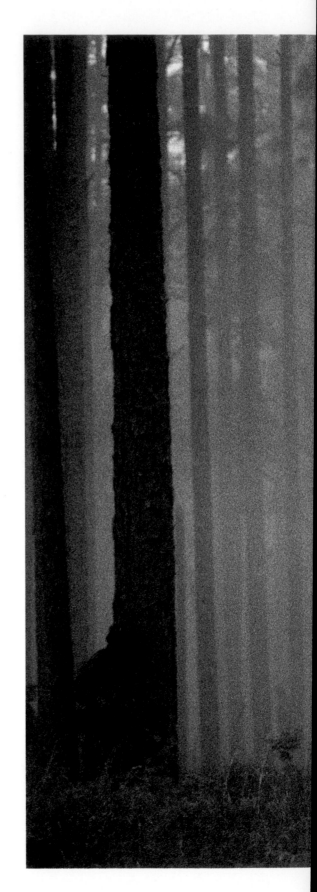

Named for Leonidas Polk, who besides being the first Episcopal bishop of the Diocese of Louisiana was also a Confederate general, Fort Polk was established in 1941 to train U.S. Army soldiers for World War II. Today the post, just outside Leesville, serves as home to the Joint Readiness Training Center for U.S. light infantry and special operations forces.

In 1869, a few years after its slaves were freed, the owners of Ashton Plantation provided them with a Baptist minister to begin a congregation. In 1888 the members built St. John the Baptist Baptist Church just north of Lecompte. It is considered the mother church of most of the African American Baptists in the area.

Facing page: The Bentley Hotel was built in the heart of downtown Alexandria in 1908 by lumber entrepreneur Joseph Bentley. Located at the physical center of the state, the Bentley became a favorite meeting place for politicians. It thrived during World War II, when some 7 million men were sent to central Louisiana for military training. Following a period of decline, the grand old neoclassical building received extensive renovation that was completed in 1985.

Easter morning at St. John the Baptist Baptist Church, just north of Lecompte. The old wooden pews creak as, under the greenish fluorescent lights, we sway to the music of the small but enthusiastic gospel choir.

Then the sermon begins. The preacher is at ease as he launches into his text—an experienced pro, slow and sure. Then, about halfway through, the rich tone of his voice changes. The words seem to be coming from a different place inside the man as they deeply resonate and gain the fire of poetry. The preacher is no longer at ease. Neither is the congregation. Emotion mounts. The story of Thomas doubting the risen Christ reaches out to grab hold of the worshipers. The inspired delivery gives the words a power that simply cannot be denied. The preacher and congregation lean toward each other in a holy communion of redemptive message.

The preacher is on a roll—he could go on far past the noon hour. But he has another church at which to deliver his Easter message. Abruptly, like the flipping of a switch, the sermon ends. He looks me in the eye from the pulpit and asks if there is anyone present who would like to introduce himself. I oblige.

Fried chicken, coleslaw, and potato salad are served in the kitchen. The members of the congregation take their lunches and gather in sunshine in the front yard for fellowship.

Amen.

Generations of Highway 1 travelers have enjoyed ham sandwiches and plate lunches with the classic southern finale at Lea's Lunchroom in Lecompte. Established in 1928 by Lea and Georgie Johnson, the diner has not been deterred by the fact that I-49 bypassed Lecompte.

A chef in Washington barbecues some serious chicken for a Saturday evening church benefit.

Facing page: Washington, on Bayou Courtableau in St. Landry Parish, was an extremely active riverboat port in the late nineteenth century. Shown here, the Nathaniel Offutt House, *circa* 1840, is an example of the historic homes that remain in the town, now known for its many antique shops.

At summer's end, the place to hear nonstop pulsating zydeco is the Zydeco Festival at Plaisance. Here, Zydeco Express pumps out the electrified blend of traditional black Creole and Cajun music with a distinctive rhythm-and-blues influence.

Facing page: Eunice's Liberty Theater, built in 1924 as a vaudeville house, now serves as the home of *Rendez-Vous des Cajuns,* a program broadcast live almost entirely in French on radio every Saturday night since 1987. The performances, such as this one by J. C. Labbie and Ses Amis Cajuns, feature primarily Cajun music and zydeco and are cosponsored by the city of Eunice and the Prairie Acadian Cultural Center of the Jean Lafitte National Historical Park and Preserve.

The soil structure and plentiful water make southwestern Louisiana ideal for growing rice. The field is flooded from seeding until just before harvest to discourage weeds. Here an underground irrigation system discharges water to maintain the proper level in this Acadia Parish rice field.

Levee systems are built in rice fields to keep the water contained at a depth of two to four inches. The field is flooded for two to three months during the growing season, then allowed to dry out for the summer harvest.

Facing page: As protein-rich soybeans are planted in this Acadia Parish field, a young man prepares a batch of seeds applying a fungicide to protect them from disease as they sprout.

Tee Mamou Mardi Gras. The name is short for *petit* ("little") Mamou, so called to distinguish it from Mamou proper, a nearby town sometimes referred to as *grand* ("big") Mamou.

The Tee Mamou flatlands are perfect for growing rice and soybeans. But on Mardi Gras morning each year—rain or shine—a group of men leave their farm implements, don colorful costumes, and grab a beer or three. The more garish the fabric and accessories for their garb, the better.

The Tee Mamou Mardi Gras bears little resemblance to the Carnival festivities in New Orleans. It is not a parade. The revelers do not throw beads, and no crowds line the rural prairie roads leading eventually into Iota. But it is very much a party on wheels. With their own Cajun band in tow, the celebrants arrive at farms begging for small change and a contribution to the community gumbo pot. At each stop a nimble but doomed chicken is released to be chased through mud and brush until caught. When the captured bird is held triumphantly aloft, the music takes over. After the all-too-brief dance, the revelers are "whipped" back onto the trailer by the captains, and the whoops and cheers recede down the road.

Overleaf: Snow geese, whose breeding habitat is the Arctic tundra of northern Canada, take wing near the Cameron Prairie National Wildlife Refuge in Cameron Parish. Coastal Louisiana, especially in the southwest where the Mississippi flyway and the Central flyway overlap, is a stopover for huge numbers of migratory birds, in part because of the vast wetlands in the state—roughly 40 percent of all coastal wetlands in America.

Rosie Ledet and the Zydeco Playboys crank out a lively dance number at Iota's Mardi Gras street festival in Acadia Parish.

Pecan grove at sunrise, Cameron Parish.

Duck hunters share a palpable passion for their sport. Because of the extensive marshlands of the state and through the work of organizations like Ducks Unlimited, which work to preserve both waterfowl and wetlands, there are between two and three million ducks in Louisiana at any given time during the winter.

In 1967, due to its drastic decline, the American alligator was placed on the endangered species list and experts were pessimistic about its chances. But populations rebounded so quickly that in 1987 the alligator was pronounced fully recovered and taken off the list. September is alligator-hunting season in Louisiana, with hunters buying state permits to take a limited number of the animals. Both the meat and hide are highly valued. Here, a woman in Gueydan (Vermilion Parish) skins a freshly caught gator.

Facing page: A stand of live oaks in Grand Coteau, St. Landry Parish.

Accordions on display during Lafayette's Festival International de Louisiane.

St. John the Evangelist Catholic Church was founded in 1821 and became a cathedral with the establishment of the Diocese of Lafayette in 1918. In the heart of Lafayette, this is the church's third structure. Built to a basilican plan, it was completed in 1916. The adjacent live oak is approximately 450 years old and is "vice-president" of the Live Oak Society.

At dawn on the Feast of All Souls, the altar in the historic cemetery behind St. John the Evangelist Cathedral is ready for mass.

Great blue heron at Lake Martin, near Breaux
Bridge.

Facing page: Lunchers in Lafayette demonstrate the
classic technique for dealing with several pounds
of boiled crawfish.

Each Good Friday, the priest from Catahoula leads
his followers in prayer at each station of the cross
along the highway between St. Martinville and
Catahoula.

Facing page: Beside St. Martin de Tours Catholic
Church in St. Martinville is a statue in memory of
Evangeline, the heroine of Longfellow's epic ro-
mantic poem about the arrival of the Acadians
(Cajuns) in Louisiana. Emmeline Labiche, supposedly the real-life model for Evangeline, is buried
elsewhere in the churchyard. The statue was donated in 1927 by the actress Dolores del Rio, who
posed for it after she portrayed Evangeline in the
movie version of the story. St. Martin de Tours,
recognized as the mother church of the Acadians,
was founded in 1765, the year they first arrived in
substantial numbers in south Louisiana. The current building dates to 1832.

Shadows-on-the-Teche, completed in 1834 by sugar planter David Weeks, became the multi-generational home of his descendants. When a great-grandson, Weeks Hall, returned from World War I, he found the old mansion empty and in disrepair. He spent much of his life restoring the building and its gardens, aided by extensive documentation of the house's history discovered in the attic. Hall died in 1958, having willed the Shadows to the National Trust for Historic Preservation. It is the only property in the state owned and operated by the trust. Nearby Bayou Teche supposedly got its name from *tenche,* an Indian word for "snake," referring to the bayou's serpentine path through the heart of Acadiana.

After sugarcane is harvested, it is sent to mills like this one in New Iberia. White steam billows continually as the juice is squeezed from the cane and boiled down. The process is call "grinding," and the harvest season is known as "grinding time" in south Louisiana.

The extremely high water table in south Louisiana makes it impossible to bury the dead below ground; hence most graves are raised. This cemetery is in Delcambre.

Sugarcane harvested near Erath in Vermilion
Parish is loaded into a cane truck for the journey
to the mill.

Upon delivery from the farm, harvested rice is
sampled at the Riviana Rice Mill in Abbeville. Raw
rice drawn into the hollow copper probe is checked
for quality before the rice is unloaded for processing into white rice for the table.

Overleaf: The sun rises over the marshes of the
Paul J. Rainey Wildlife Sanctuary in Vermilion
Parish. Donated in 1924, this is the oldest and
largest sanctuary of the National Audubon Society.

A shrimp boat puts out its nets off Marsh Island.

Facing page: Cane fields verge on a sugar mill at Franklin.

A boater steers a channel in the Atchafalaya Basin. The Basin was once thought to be worthless swamp, and much of it was drained and cleared for farmland. Today, the 1.4-million-acre wetland, teaming with wildlife, is recognized as a national ecological treasure.

Facing page: Left to its own, the Mississippi River would change course and pour its waters down the Atchafalaya River. This, the second of two Old River Control Structures that have been built in lower Concordia Parish, regulates the Mississippi by diverting controlled amounts of its flow down the Atchafalaya. The Army Corps of Engineers' lower Mississippi River flood-control project, the largest project of the Corps, also includes the Morganza Control Structure, the Bonnet Carré Spillway, and the extensive levee system.

A great egret takes breakfast-to-go in the Atchafalaya Basin.

Facing page: A bald eagle witnesses sunrise from his perch on a cypress in the Atchafalaya Basin.

Blue iris in the Atchafalaya Basin.

The Atchafalaya wetlands contain roughly a billion crawfish, presenting a bountiful spring harvest for crawfishermen like this one. Live crawfish are normally greenish brown, but a splash in the boiling pot turns them a deep, appetizing red.

Greenwood, a cotton and sugarcane plantation, was built in 1830 in northern West Feliciana Parish by William Ruffin Barrow. The home was struck by lightning and burned to its foundations in 1960. Beginning in 1968 with the help of numerous photographs of the house's interior and exterior, a new owner meticulously restored Greenwood.

Built in 1794 on a Spanish land grant, The Myrtles was extensively renovated by two successive sets of owners after 1975. The front gallery (porch) of the house is 120 feet long. The Myrtles is north of St. Francisville in an area noted for its many surviving antebellum plantation homes.

Built in 1806 on a cotton plantation near St. Francisville, Oakley with its British Creole architecture is now part of the Audubon State Commemorative Area. John James Audubon worked on his now-famous *Birds of America* series while employed here as a tutor in 1821.

Oakley's garden from within the house.

Port Hudson, just north of Baton Rouge, was the last Confederate stronghold on the Mississippi River, built to complement the defenses at Vicksburg to keep the vital waterway from complete Union control. The longest true siege of the Civil War took place here. After forty-eight days and two ferocious but failed Union attempts to break through the breastworks, the Confederate garrison surrendered on July 9, 1863, five days after the fall of Vicksburg.

Scott's Bluff, at the north Baton Rouge campus of
Southern University, provides this spectacular view
of the Mississippi River.

In 1846, Louisiana's legislature voted to move the state government out of New Orleans, a city that many rural legislators castigated as exerting immoral influences. On the other hand, it appears that few of the lawmakers wanted to be *too* far from the temptations of the metropolis, as they selected Baton Rouge, an easy steamboat ride upriver, as the new seat of government.

The first structure to house the state government in Baton Rouge is now called the Old State Capitol. Architect James Dakin designed it in a neo-Gothic style to resemble a castle. Pictured is the central staircase of the then-controversial building. The capitol was gutted by fire during the Civil War but renovated in the early 1880s. There was a period of neglect after the New State Capitol opened, but a four-year renovation completed in 1994 has turned the old building into a showplace that also contains a museum of Louisiana politics.

91

The Louisiana House of Representatives in session.

Facing page: Sunrise greets the New State Capitol, built during the tenure of Huey P. Long, who revolutionized Louisiana from his election as governor in 1928 until his assassination in this building in 1935, when he was a United States senator. The new capitol was designed by the New Orleans architectural firm of Weiss, Dreyfous, and Seiferth, and dedicated in 1932. Long was buried in the center of the building's formal gardens. A monument to him, erected in 1940, marks the gravesite.

Overleaf: Louisiana State University, the state's flagship university, originated as the State Seminary of Learning and Military Academy in Rapides Parish. The school was moved to Baton Rouge in 1869 and renamed Louisiana State University the following year. The present campus, begun by Governor John M. Parker, opened in 1925 with 1,712 students. The campus architect, Theodore Link, chose the North Italian Renaissance style, including the distinctive red tile roofs.

Game night in Tiger Stadium reverberates with an
energy felt almost statewide. The stadium's first
game was played against Tulane on Thanksgiving
Day in 1924—the year before LSU's new south
Baton Rouge campus itself was opened. A crowd of
18,000—the largest ever to have watched a football
game in Louisiana at that time—jammed the not-
fully-completed stands. Today, after many
enlargements, the stadium seats almost 80,000.

Exxon's Baton Rouge refinery, on the banks of the Mississippi just north of downtown, turns out a variety of petroleum products and ships them worldwide. Constructed in a cotton field in 1909, Standard Oil's original refinery was once the largest in the world. Exxon's present-day petrochemical complex, with more than 4,000 employees, remains major force in the local economy.

Mile Branch Settlement was established in 1976 as a tribute to the nineteenth-century settlers of Washington Parish. Each individual structure was donated, moved to this site in Franklinton adjacent to the Washington Parish Free Fair, and then restored for living-history presentations.

The rolling hills and wide-open spaces of St. Tam-
many Parish are the setting for a center of the
state's sport-horse industry. These young thor-
oughbreds belong to Oak Hill Ranch, one of many
horse farms that dot the countryside surrounding
Folsom.

April is strawberry harvest month outside Independence in Tangipahoa Parish.

Statues at roadside sale in Tickfaw, Tangipahoa
Parish.

Not every home in Manchac Swamp has a road leading up to it. Most of the swamp, which lies roughly between Lakes Maurepas and Pontchartrain, is accessible only by water. Manchac constitutes a major wilderness resource literally within sight of New Orleans.

Facing page: Springing up in the 1850s as a stop on the New Orleans–Jackson Railroad, Ponchatoula was completely destroyed only a few years later by Union troops during the Civil War. The Tangipahoa Parish town later became a center for logging, and then for strawberry growing. Today it also markets history as an antique haven.

A veteran campaigner in Manchac Swamp.

In 1894, what is now the Gillis W. Long Hansen's Disease Center near Carville was established as a state institution for patients with what was then known as leprosy. Two years later the Daughters of Charity of St. Vincent de Paul took it over. In 1921 it was transferred to federal jurisdiction and is now known internationally for its treatment, rehabilitation, and research services.

Nottoway Plantation, the largest antebellum plantation home in the South, is a blend of Greek-revival and Italianate architecture. Built in 1859 by Henry Howard for owner John Hampden Randolph, the home features 64 rooms. It stands just north of White Castle in Iberville Parish.

Overleaf: Nottoway.

This stunning house at Vacherie in St. James Parish was built in 1805 for Guillaume DuParc. It became "Laura" in 1891, when great-granddaughter Laura Duparc Locoul sold part of the property on condition that her name be given to it. The bright colors are reminiscent of those favored by early Creole planters for their homes.

Oak Alley, upriver from Vacherie, is one of the best
examples of the Greek-revival architectural style
that was in vogue among builders of plantation
homes along the Mississippi during the mid-1800s.
Completed in 1839, it is famed for its alley of
twenty-eight live oak trees. The oaks are believed
to have been planted by a settler in the early 1700s,
making them nearly a century older than the house
they now frame.

The Mississippi River is the superhighway of American river traffic.

On one trip between Baton Rouge and New Orleans, I happened upon barricades before the brand-new Veterans Bridge at Gramercy. The bridge was completed but not yet open to traffic. At the apex of the massive structure, I stood at the railing and spent a sublime morning becoming one with the Mississippi River.

A distant freighter coming downstream caught my eye. The swift current brought it quickly into the foreground, giving me surprisingly little time to expose several frames before the huge vessel slipped out of sight under the bridge. I hopped the center barrier and ran to the downstream railing. The gigantic craft launched itself soundlessly into view directly below me. Time stopped. I shivered at the sheer immensity of the ship and how such an object could move so fast and so silently. And then it hit me. It isn't the ship at all. It is the river. The ship is a mere child's plaything floating atop the almost unimaginable force of the river itself.

Facing page: The Veterans Memorial Bridge over the Mississippi looms behind a field of sugarcane that provides a lush backdrop to a small cemetery just downriver from Vacherie. By long custom, the gravesites are cleaned up and adorned with flowers on All Saints' Day.

A string of refineries, chemical plants, and similar facilities lines the banks of the Mississippi from Baton Rouge to New Orleans, forming one of the world's major industrial corridors. Shown here is the Kaiser Aluminum plant near Gramercy.

View from Veterans Memorial Bridge on the west bank. The highway below is Louisiana's historic River Road (actually two roads, one on each side of the Mississippi), parts of which were first carved out in colonial times.

Each December traditional log structures are carefully constructed along the levees between Baton Rouge and New Orleans, then set ablaze on Christmas Eve. The adjacent towns of Gramercy and Lutcher in St. James Parish sponsor the Bonfires on the Levee Festival, during which hundreds of bonfires light the riverbank for miles.

The ladies' parlor at San Francisco.

Completed in 1856, San Francisco was the main house for Edmond Marmillion's sugar plantation. His Bavarian daughter-in-law, Louise von Seybold, was responsible for the distinctive Bavarian colors of the house. Tall cisterns flank the "steamboat Gothic" structure, set on the east bank of the Mississippi River in St. John the Baptist Parish just upstream from New Orleans.

Alligators, no longer endangered in Louisiana, not only thrive in the state's wetlands but also are grown commercially on "alligator farms," such as this one near Galliano.

Feeding time for a large resident of a gator farm.

Shrimp boats at the town of Cut Off, on Bayou
Lafourche.

At Port Fourchon, near the mouth of Bayou Lafourche, it can be difficult to say just where the marshland ends and the Gulf begins.

Facing the open waters of the Gulf of Mexico and evidence of oil exploration both present and past, these anglers hope to hook redfish near Port Four-chon. The concrete breakwater system was installed to impede erosion by storm-driven waves.

Overleaf: Everything a fisherman might want can be found on Grand Isle. The island, at the end of Highway 1, hosts the world-class Grand Isle International Tarpon Rodeo each July.

The *Ocean Valiant* probes for oil in the Gulf.

Venice is the end of the road below New Orleans. From there our helicopter cruised south at a hundred miles per hour for thirty minutes. The horizontal fountain of brown Mississippi River silt disgorging into the blue Gulf quickly disappeared behind us. Before us lay the Ocean Valiant, *a structure part island, part vessel. The state-of-the-art third-generation semisubmersible drilling rig, hired out to explore for oil at Texaco's Genesis Prospect, floated more than 3,300 feet from the ocean floor, secured by cables stretching four different directions.*

Within minutes after the chopper settled down on the pad, I found myself atop the rig's tower, breathing a warm November breeze and searching the horizon for anything other than blue-on-blue water reflecting billowy white clouds. Aside from one distant, disconnected freighter steaming by, I finally spotted one other rig many miles away. The men and women aboard the Ocean Valiant *are alone, true explorers in the energy business.*

I know that on some days the winds and waves turn evil, but the day of my visit was glorious, and my feet literally dragged as we walked to the elevator to descend from our perch to the rig floor below.

Once extinct in Louisiana even though it is the official state bird, the brown pelican has been successfully reestablished from the Florida population.

Venice is literally the end of the road along the Mississippi River below New Orleans. Travelers heading farther downstream go by boat or helicopter. The town exists to support offshore oil and gas exploration as well as commercial and sports fishing.

Plaquemines Parish supports a citrus industry, featuring the prized Satsuma and navel oranges.

Traffic on the Mississippi River is not all tankers, freighters, and towboats pushing barges. Many pleasure boats, including cruise liners such as this one, share the waterway.

Facing page: An empty Victorian home in Pointe à la Hache, a Mississippi River town in the heart of Plaquemines Parish.

New Orleans is called the Crescent City for its location on a sweeping bend of the Mississippi River.
The city was founded by Jean Baptiste Le Moyne,
sieur de Bienville, in 1718. In 1722 the raw little
settlement replaced Mobile as the capital of
France's Louisiana colony.

A ferry from New Orleans approaches the community of Algiers on the west bank of the Mississippi.

New Orleans' public-transportation system was
established in 1835 in the form of mule-drawn
omnibuses. By the 1850s the vehicles ran on rails
and were either pulled by horses and mules or
powered by steam. Electric streetcars arrived in
1893 and at one time served virtually all of the city.
Today the single route that remains, from Canal
Street up the length of St. Charles Avenue and part
of Carrollton Avenue, is the oldest continuously
operating streetcar line in the world.

The stately homes along the quiet, shady streets of the Garden District echo the distant time when cotton, sugar, and shipping wealth made New Orleans the Queen City of the South. Many of the houses were built in the antebellum period in the Greek-revival style then popular. Many newly arrived Anglo-Americans settled in the area, giving it a different character from that of the French Quarter. The name "Garden District" may have arisen from the fact that the houses here had large yards, often with flower gardens, whereas in the Vieux Carré houses were built flush to the sidewalks and had plantings only in their interior courtyards.

Each Tuesday night, the Rebirth Brass Band takes
the stage to blow the tin-paneled walls off uptown's
Maple Leaf Bar with a combination of funk and
traditional street jazz.

Facing page: The Camellia Grill opened at St.
Charles and Carrollton in 1946, and the traditional
diner has since established itself as a New Orleans
institution.

The Louisiana Superdome is where the New Orleans Saints battle visiting NFL teams, and is a frequent setting for the Super Bowl.

Facing page: In December, City Park is bedecked with thousands upon thousands of lights for the annual Celebration in the Oaks. Driving and walking tours are offered in this, the fifth-largest urban park in America.

Overleaf: Commander's Palace, New Orleans.

*N*ew Orleans is music and New Orleans is food. When one brings up the subject of dining in the Crescent City, there is the danger that the discussion could go on for days. Luckily, comparing New Orleans restaurants is not a contact sport—not often, at least.

Founded in the Garden District by Emile Commander in 1880, Commander's Palace quickly became and remains a favorite dining destination of New Orleanians and knowledgeable visitors. After a tour of the full-blast kitchen bursting with a glorious cacophony of smells, I went to the roof to photograph the restaurant's elegant courtyard from above. From that perspective I was privileged to witness an hour of choreography performed by the waiters, their movements studied, smooth, and utterly unobtrusive, so as not to draw the slightest attention away from the pleasure of the dining experience. Some skills, honed to perfection, become essentially invisible.

Other skills, such those performed over a hot stove, are the opposite. They can overwhelm and confuse the diner. Is he or she in heaven or in danger of hell for tasting something so sinfully exquisite? Such is dining at Commander's and many other New Orleans restaurants.

As I left, a genuinely surprised waiter asked me, "You're not eating before you go?" People to see, places to be. So sad.

"Throw me something, mister!" The traditional shout and a forest of hands beg the krewe of Zulu for Carnival throws—plastic beads, "doubloons," and drinking cups flung profusely from the parade floats and coveted as treasures by the streetside crowds. Zulu's trademark gold-coconut throws are among the most favored of all.

Facing page: Mardi Gras—or more properly, Carnival—is a season of celebration and revelry traditionally beginning on January 6 and culminating on the night before Ash Wednesday. Parades and masked balls occur almost without letup in New Orleans and its suburbs during that time, but Fat Tuesday itself, when the parades of Rex and Zulu roll back-to-back, is when the crowds are thickest, the noise the loudest, and the atmosphere the most festive.

The Mardi Gras Indians hit the streets of New Orleans on Mardi Gras Day displaying feathered costumes that are both intricate and extravagant. The tradition supposedly arose partly from the influence of traveling Wild West Shows; if so, it has long since taken on an exuberant life of its own.

The Café Du Monde is a place to sip café au lait, nibble beignets (square, holeless doughnuts), and watch the twenty-four-hour street life of the Vieux Carré.

Jackson Square is the center of the Vieux Carré ("Old Square") or French Quarter, which ironically contains only one truly French building. Two massive fires, in 1788 and 1794, destroyed everything but the Ursuline Convent (1750), which survived because it sat somewhat apart from other structures. The Cabildo (on the left here) was built by the Spanish in 1795. St. Louis Cathedral, the best-known landmark in the Quarter, is the third church on the site and dates to 1851.

Facing page: Elaborate ironwork, such as this oak leaf and acorn pattern, figures prominently in French Quarter architecture.

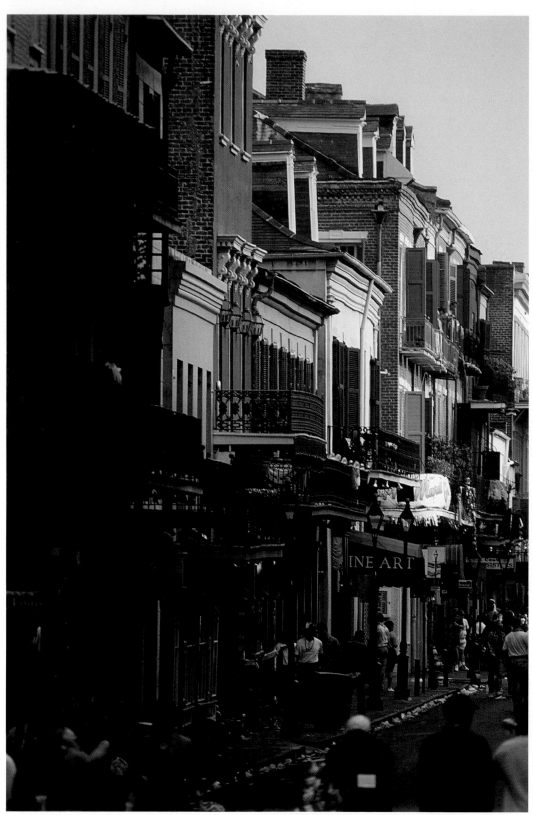

Royal Street, a center for artworks and antiques.

With British troops threatening New Orleans in the last days of the War of 1812, General Andrew Jackson called upon the people of the city to help defend it. With a motley army of soldiers and volunteers, including cannoneers from the pirate Jean Lafitte's crew, the outnumbered Americans defeated the enemy in the climactic battle of January 8, 1815, six miles downriver at Chalmette. Unknown to everyone, envoys in Europe had two weeks earlier signed a treaty ending the war.

Clarence Johnson plays clarinet for Greg Stafford and the Jazz Hounds at the Palm Court Jazz Café. Growing out of the music and rhythms of the blue-collar population, which in New Orleans included Italian, German, Irish, West African, and Caribbean cultures, jazz took hold and flourished in the city, then spread to the rest of the nation and the world.

Facing page: Hanging out and hanging on in the French Quarter.

146

French Quarter courtyard.

INDEX